GW01034093

THE NOISE
OF
MASONRY SETTLING

First published in 2006 by
The Dedalus Press
13 Moyclare Road
Baldoyle
Dublin 13
Ireland

www.dedaluspress.com

© Leland Bardwell, 2006

All rights reserved. No part of this publication may be reproduced in any form or by any means without the prior permission of the publisher.

ISBN 1 904556 44 2 (paper)

Dedalus Press titles are represented and distributed in the USA and Canada by Dufour Editions Ltd., PO Box 7, Chester Springs, Pennsylvania 19425, and in the UK by Central Books, 99 Wallis Road, London E9 5LN

Front cover image by Michael Boran
Design by Pat Boran

Printed and bound in the UK by Lightning Source, 6 Precedent Drive, Rooksley, Milton Keynes MK13 8PR, UK

The Dedalus Press receives financial assistance from
An Chomhairle Ealaíon / The Arts Council, Ireland

THE NOISE
OF
MASONRY SETTLING

Leland Bardwell

AUTHOR'S NOTE

I wish to express my thanks to Mary Branley for her patience in reading the manuscript in embryo, to the poets Eilean Ní Chuilleanáin and Macdara Woods for their friendship and encouragement down the years, and to my editor and publisher, Pat Boran.

— Leland Bardwell

ACKNOWLEDGEMENTS

Grateful acknowledgement is made to the editors of the following in which many of the poems in this collection have previously appeared:

Aquarius, Arena, Cyphers, The Holy Door and *The Shop*. For those poems which have been translated into Polish, Hungarian, German, French, Hebrew and Spanish, the author would like to thank her various translators.

To my six children
and numerous grandchildren,
with thanks for just being there

Contents

The Knowledge of Beezie McGowan

She knows where the whelks gather,
The booty of waves,
The mussels.

She knows where the limpets lie,
How the rocks
Are spreading.

She knows where the dilisk hides
In the pitted cracks
When the water's ebbing.

She can tell the storm
By the heron's flight
From cliff to harbour,

But wages were poor
In this industry of God's,
The learning got so hard, so hard.

Moving House

The house unfolds and straightens with relief.
We've discarded the stone, the elephant,
the Japanese parasol and the pile
of unfinished poems.
They are like rotten fruit,
might be a core worth extracting.

Are you taking the piano? Yes.
The mice are nesting in the keys
And sit with paws crossed like expectant choirboys.

We are tired of this move
And all the other moves we've made,
And tired of the people who are tired
Of carting memories around.

The magic of summer took us by the neck
And wrung us out like an old sock.
Is it possible we've accumulated
So much rubbish in so short a time?

Let us go then quickly before dark.
In this way we'll close the shutters of absence
And find a new set of attachments and trivia.

'These Aspirins Seem To Be No Use' —
*Last Words of Ernest Shakleton, Died of Angina Pectoris,
January 4th, 1922*

for my cousin Robbie

What possessed you
On that last trip, sucking on the fags,
Drinking champagne by the neck,
Imagining your poor heart
Could get you there and back?

As your heart couldn't follow,
You followed it
Like all great explorers—
Emily Brontë, saying
'You can send for the doctor now,'
Tolstoy, doing press-ups
at the railway station,
Flaubert wishing
He hadn't written *Madame Bovary*...

Maybe it's the pure whiteness
The spirit needs
That drives one on in the end.

I'll Do the Messages

I'll do the messages,
Give me the poison drops
From the orphan's tongue.
I'll pre-digest the wrong.

I'll sell the flags for the flag-seller
And hold the tiresome horse
For the smith with four dead wives.

The apple is in your side, my brother.
I'll learn the Blue Danube
From the village dressmaker.
I am the scape-goat and I'll dance
To someone else's tune.

Ten tall sunflowers grew in my garden.
They played the incomparable artist's game:
One black eye each and a dart
That was the start of my garden.

I walked through the trees of adolescence,
The angry walnut and sheltering beech.
A seed was sown in an ebony heart.
Let the bud decide where the flower shall fall.

Hard to Imagine Your Face Dead

Hard to imagine your face dead,
Not giving out, pontificating,
Just quiet, serene, the moustache resting
Over the broken tooth.

Those eyes—no longer
Like water brimming
Over a gutter caught with sun.

Your shoulders, no longer alert
In your cushion of death,
Their anger subsiding.

Better to imagine you lying
Alone and listless,
Like when the speed used to leave you
In the downbeat of your madness.

For Dermot and Anne Marie
on Attending the Birth of Dallan

Pimlico and Vauxhall Bridge
And that sally-port near the Tate
Where barges lie deck to deck
Like lesbians, and Blake
Has burnt Satan in Milton's house.

Tantalus up to his waist
in the Thames can't drink,
though the water leans on his thighs.
Pimlico and Eleanor Rigby
At the end of the Chelsea game.

Pimlico and splinter city
Jostle for life under cranes.
'Bow down to the artists,
those birds have no wings, boy,
they sing for their supper.'

Pimlico and Adam's rib
Have put their names on the list.
The morainic wastes are groaning
At the end of the map,
But the compass is spinning.

In Pimlico live Harlequin
and cat—look fast for the
shadows they leave. Citizens stir
in their sleep, and Hesperus
sneaks shrough the grimy window.

In Pimlico the lending library
Lies on the hem of Cat's hair
On the pillow; the hazel strand
Is the margin of waiting allowed,
Like the whiskey dream of slow water spreading.

Where the Grass is Dark with Trees
for Dan

I want to walk in the field
Where the grass is dark with trees

I want to take the hand of the past
As round and clean as an autumn apple

And hold it tight as a nail
Till all the talking is done

For the seabird's cry is still the saddest

Lobster Fishing

Lend me your education,
Glum Clare man,
While your sockless boots
Slide on the algae

Under the jawbone of cliff,
Whipped by the anxious sleeves of wind.
The night air burns with salt.
The cliffs shout back at the sea,
Their gun-metal mouths
Hungry for lacey kisses.

We have eased ourselves down,
Promoted the cliff-stairs to safe passage
Above the sea-howl, each step
Widening on to the outcrop of armoured rock
Making its individual sound as the sea-plants crack,
'Beach the bloody crates!'

Orders is orders
For he is no crazy man: pots are expensive,
A living must be got.
His anger swings in the storm like a metal moon.
No caution allowed
In these recondite surroundings.

It was fighting for hours, it seemed,
The wet ropes rasping already frozen fingers
Till crowding back on the baize shelves of Kilbaha
The crates are counted. Six. All safe.
He is exultant. The ocean swell behind us
We'll go to Killrush and later cash the cheque.

Yet for me, when the thin line of dawn
Splinters the kitchen window,
I am concious of a poor green thing
Too small to sell and ready for the pot.

I should much prefer to tie it on a string
And prance upon a street
Mindful of Gerard de Nerval.

Oh Well! (de mortuis... etc)

Climbing the spinal steps,
The vertebraic ladder,
The fieldmouse of panic
Creeps silently

In the heel of night,
The skin of her anger
Racing from terminal to terminal,
Dodging and doubling back
From the campanology
Of the mortuary doors.

Gráinne dragging fishtails
To the mountain cave.

The West's Asleep

Death comes handy, they say,
When the leaf snaps,
Sleeps and stalks back,
When the bud quickens.
Two months that bring up the toll.

As the years pass
The houses empty.
No light shines from the windows,
No dogs bark on the long road
That hangs from Cloonagh.

A straggling beard
Of ragweed, thistle, goosefoot,
And the wild cup of the rose
Calls out the names:
Tom, The Black Doctor,
Ellie, Sarah, Jack.
Ah sure,
They're all gone now
And none to come after.

That Day

Either
Daryl V. Zanuch or
Cecil B. De Mille
Said, *I employed*
Gary Cooper
The day
He got old.

Can ordinary people,
Who are not
Film directors
Recognise that day
Without being told?

Office Vignette

Mr. Blank sat on his office stool
Dictating to Miss Brazen
The beauties of profit.
'Screw me,' she said,
When she came to the billion pound paragraph.
He did, on the edge-to-edge.
Unscrewed, she resumed her task.
Miss Flower, on the other hand,
The artistic type, couldn't bear it.
So much pink flesh on the carpet,
So much force against the waste-paper basket,
So much paper on the floor,
And all because of
The high interest rate regime
In the corollary of a falling currency.
Mr. Blank sat on his office stool
Looking at Miss Flower.
He was expecting rain.

My Brother Reggie

My brother Reggie
Was generous with epithets—
Face-Ache, Vim Tin, Toast-Rack—
Not without a trace
Of humour. Why not let
Me be Maid of the Track?
I asked. It did not
Crack his face.

My brother Reggie
Liked to put the pillow
Over my head, and press,
Press down so
Till my head was flat.
He said, *I want you dead.*
But what fun is there in that?

My Brother Reggie,
A gentleman to his guts,
Is a hundred years old
And hedges his bets.
He doesn't care to put
His hands round my throat
And squeeze me weird.
Like a goat,
He just hugs his beard.

Love Poem

The nicest thing
You ever said to me
Was
Do we always have to live
Like Bonnie and Clyde?

The Night's Empty Shells

I am always afraid
They will find me
Like the skinned arm of the child,

Break the joint between
The ulna and the radius,
Gouge out the mephitic matter,

Take the dance from my feet,
Splay the small bones,
Work the cement into the instep
Before I have settled the measure.

I am not here to ogle the sea,
Count the brent geese,
On the short strand below Ardtrasna,

I'm here to learn the light of Lislarry
Where shone the shebeen once:
A fisherman's star.

So sailed Praeger
After breakfast of poitín
And cold potatoes—a note

To the waves—a leaky boat,
A nod to the dawn
On the East of Innismurray.

For once on my gable
A beacon shone,
The end of the sea lane

To a safe hauling
Of the night's empty shells.

Heart Trouble

It was the heart, after all,
That let her down.
So she lay under the frown
Of the cardiologist,
Thinking:
At least this is respectable.
It might have been me found
Dead drunk in someone else's kitchen.

Innismurray

'Where there's a cow there's a woman and where there's a woman, there's mischief' — St Colmcille who founded the monastery and banned all cows from the island

Two thumb holes in the birthing stone
Beside the women's graveyard.

There she squats, prayers
Breaking from parched lips

To the great Man-God to deliver her
From the yearly gall of labour,

To beg for a man-child
To erase the guilt of her sex.

For being a woman
Has no pardon,

Skirts raised in the wind
On an island that floats

Like a bayleaf
In the unforgiving sea.

She crouches thus
Till the infant lies in the skutch

And she looks at the unmarked grave
Beneath whose soil her mother lies.

She ponders.

We Don't Serve Travelling People

The barman attacks the counter,
His dry cloth bolting in fury
Along the plastic beam.
His eyes like electric studs
Fasten on to me.

I feel the familiar pain.

We don't serve travelling people
Or prostitutes.

No, I am not popular in pubs.
Nine out of ten times I hear
That icy 'madam' cast upon the shore
Of my uncomplaining retreat.

Not here not there-—from Liffey Street
To Donnybrook and back—
There's nowhere left, it seems,
To rest the prostitution
Of my weary but travelling mind.

'No Road Beyond the Graveyard'

—Chief Inspector Morse in a novel by Colin Dexter

But the No Road beyond the graveyard
Is full of possibilities,
Eidetic visions, ghosts,
The valedictory sigh, perhaps.
But when I stand on this No Road,
I am thinking of an old woman
Who took the shoes of her son
And polished them, polished them,
Till you could see your face in them,
First the left, then the right,
And placed them under the kitchen table
Before she died. And the son
Stands at the No Road
In the dulled shoes,
In a hopeless frame of mind.
There's no reason for this No Road.
No mention of falling stones,
Dangerous cliffs
Likely to flood.
Simply No Road,
No five-barred gate,
No 'Dogs Keep Out',
No 'Danger Men at Work',
No 'Closed for Repair',
Just, beyond the graveyard,
'No Road'.
No cul de sac, no boreen
No bridle path.
The road doesn't go nowhere,
It simply isn't.

It's quiet too in the graveyard
No creature, no bird,
No field mouse. Quiet.
Rows upon rows of stones
Crosses, inscriptions, dates,
But quiet. In the end
One keeps one's ghosts
To oneself.

Hawthornden Castle

These forces on the battlements
Make snakes pass through her bloodstream.
Lecherous ghosts torment her
With the hooting
Of the distant owl. She cannot sleep
On this moonlit plain
To the ticking of the Rosewell mine,
The town ill-named with its stumpy streets,
Mean houses pasted over
With a coal-dust sheen.
She remembers, too, the hedgehog,
Lifeless, lying
Like a discarded gardener's glove.

Drum Up a Poem

Drum up a poem,
They said, *for Eddie's birthday,*
And me as empty as
An upturned barrell.

Who then is this
Aquarius fellow,
This Eddie Linden?
Is he some sort
Of astronaut
In the bend of the wind
That the poor folks
Like us remember
Who did demons for us
As we struggled to climb
On to the empty page?

Good luck, so.

To the beat
Of your Irish
Sottish heart
From this upturned barrell
I send you
A drum of delight.

Cherry Blossom Again

Cherry blossom falls again
From the tree. Spring
Has drifted away and old age
Drags around me.
Why did sense pass me by
Without a primrose of recognition?

Will I never emerge from the reel
Of the ring, till the enchanted earth
Smiles cynically?
Will the mist always hide the garden from me?

Old People's Outing: Ageism

The old man on the telly
At the old people's outing
Was smiling but not breathing.
He was dressed in women's clothes.

The compère had dressed all the old men
In women's clothes,
Rolled up their pants to expose
Their soiled long-johns.
Fun, they yelled loudly.
This is real fun, they cackled
To keep the shudder of death away
But the one old man
Smiled hopelessly.
He had, for the last time,
Made a fool of himself.

Block

To beat the block
She painted dried flowers,
Baked bread,
Put wine in the Borsch,
Read *Finnegans Wake,*
But still her mind was as flat as Hungary.
'I need to fall in love,
I need pain,' she cried,
'Real pain.
Not just bad news on the telephone.'

The Lady Who Went on Strike Outside The Iveagh Hostel Because of its Early Closing Hours

I am Lily, comfy, leave
Me alone. My daft umbrellas
Shelter me. My mattress
Shapes my bones.

You can have old pin-
Stripe and his lock-up
Face in the Iveagh.

Why should I snuff
His candle light
And blow his dandelion clock?
The Liberties is my domain.
My carpet runs from Thomas Street
To St. Nicholas Without.

I lie here from Monday to Sunday.
My street's my Alphabet Walk.
I have a god-room
On this leaning street and
Love on my tree like ivy.
I am Lily, comfy, live or die.

Ghost Child Runs

The top of my house succumbed to fire,
Slates lie where they fell,
A bay window at the side
Swings on one hinge
Like the tongue of a famine child.
The room I slept in staggers
Under the ceiling-weight of rubble.
I can feel the noise of masonry settling
As the fire raced through its innards—
With casualties of floor
And ceiling, joist and window frame.

I burrow through basement
And drawing room— cyclamen wallpaper
Shrouds my shoulders or falls dog-eared
Into folds of heavy dust.
Two bats flash past—a spitting sound,
The radar of childhood quickens.

Going back (home) after forty years
May be a mistake, for now
The tall bay horse, coat dark as wine,
Stands, straddle-legged on the gravel.
A short walk to the spent wood
That runs crooked into the stream
Beyond Durkin's yard... The tall horse
Stamps its unshod hooves
Like gloved hands knocking
On the powdery wood
Of the old hall door. Mr. Durkin
Too, is long long dead—a man for books,
No time to tie his laces
Or straighten his aching back.
Ghost horse, ghost man, ghost child runs.

The Grave Digger

He came, saying
'Keep it Country',
Clint Eastwood riding
The stacks. 'It smells sweet
Up here in the cemetery.'

He said, 'Neighbour,
I'm country,
And that's the seventh dug.
It's a bad November.'

He came into the pit,
Earth and all. They took
The mule-train fast
The wires zinged,
A gorse fire raged.
'No putting it out
In this class of wind
Though it's from the West and sweet.'

Morning she heard the horse
Shake its bit, the harness clang.
She wondered about the sea,
Would the star-cold water
Suffice to cool her thighs?

A Paean for My Uncle Kit Who Died Before I Was Born

What did you think of
All those years
Pegging away in the mines?

Just a little short of breath,
you wrote, a touch of miner's
phthisis, nothing much

after seven years below.
Many men die after three,
that's what you wrote

from Benoni, Transvaal
in 1917 and three years later,
you were dead.

The price of diamonds fell,
And you all went out on strike
What was it? A drunken brawl?

Did you hit your head
On the edge of the pavement?
Did someone say:

'What's he doing there
Lying in the muck?'
An old young man of thirty -five,

Why did you go to Africa to die?
What did they tell you, your family?
That you were too wild

Too dangerously wild
For their Protestant
Mores? Too eccentric?

Did you tell them, 'So I'll go
Seek my fortune elsewhere
If I'm a nuisance here.'

The Black sheep dragging
The family down,
Did you embarrass them

With your curly locks
So beautifully portrayed
By Orpen when you were a boy.

You were full of wonder then,
As later you must have been
All those years so far from home,

Those seven long years
In the dark African tunnels,
Wondering what brought you there.

But you took your wonder with you
Nearly as far as man can go
And closed the book on it.

They didn't write to you.
They tore up all your letters.
Only a single one survived.

You were my favourite uncle
Although we never met.
Your face plays on the lute

Of my imagination,
The one friend out of all
I might have had.

The Ballad of the Fisherman's Wife

She brushed the salty weeping from her cheekbones,
Thrown by the feathered heaving of the spray.
She stubbed her toe against the herring boxes.
Death is different, it keeps away.

The silver dropped from beaks of flying seagulls,
The swell is rising. Someone ought to say
That harbour symbols cause a crazy freedom
And death is different, it keeps away,

An empty sack! She wandered off
Back to her semi-detached along the quay.
Her rage subsided like over-watered flowers.
Death is different, it keeps away.

Parchment fingers printed against the window.
'The boat is late,' she whispered, 'Keep away.'
'But I'll come in and prove that nothing alters
Death. It's different, it keeps away."

She took the 'Foreign Missions' from the dresser.
She took a fiver out of last week's pay.
'Bring bread and wine and spirits, then,' she ordered.
'Death is different, it keeps away.'

Innocents

In B Movies
They use tomato ketchup.
In art films
They use expensive
Cosmetic paint,
Not even obtainable in Ireland.

In real life
They use blood.

Bag Lady

I knew her when she was a bag lady.
She trundled places like the North Circular Road,
O'Connell Street and Fairview,
Followed the Liffey, a restless bone,
Lay down under the lid of Clery's.
But when she knew the eyes of the orphans
Had left her, she folded her briefcase
And took the long dark highway
That had always beckoned.

Barnacles

Irish Sea north westerly 7 or 8
Increasing 10 for a time
Shannon Rockall northerly
Increasing north backing northwest
Dogger Cromarty Viking
Malin Hebrides.
Doors bang, buckets race
Down the field, my skirt
Wraps round me
Like a sari. Gulls lift
And scatter like paper.
A boat bobs like a bead
As a shoulder lifts
And rolls in with a shrug.
And then the thrash of wings.
It is six o'clock, the island calls,
And the geese face into the gale,
A cardiograph in the sky...

Insomnia

With me in my truckle bed
There is a hound
A hound in my head
There is no gainsaying it
It howls

It is the lessons of darkness

Oh Couperin
Couperin Le Grand

Pigeon Outside the Dead Woman's House

Like a casual passer-by
She strolls, her shawl
Of feathers neatly pinned.

Outside Theresa's cottage
She picks at the crumbs
Of the old woman's soul.

Maybe takes it on loan.
When life peters out like that
There's no certainty

Of who is who, whether
Theresa is the pigeon
Or the pigeon is Theresa.

It is true that Theresa,
When still living,
Gazed at the island,

The island of her birth
Perhaps thinking
Were I a bird

I'd give it a peck,
A peck of a kiss,
Just there and back.

So maybe the pigeon
Is just hanging around
For instructions.

Maugherow Movements

He repeated the word *Duvet*
As though it were a charm.
Duvet, he said, curling his socks
Around her feet.

The Invisible from the USA to Iraq

We are too late again.
We have to get our bearings
In the gutter.

The sky is dark.
The birds assemble—
A murder of crows.

We dream of justice
Where a pride of lawyers
Tumbles through our brains.

We must take action, we say,
Against the invisible.
It thinks it has us trapped.

It likes to set pipebombs
For unsuspecting children
As it shouts out loudly:

'She's only a girl-woman
Crying on the sofa.'

The Song of the Whale

And the whale beached
In Lislarry. And they brought the JCB
And buried it. All thirty foot of it.
They said it was black,
Shining skin from the sea.
Grey blue, some argued
All thirty foot of it.
And the whale men came,
They came all the way from Cork,
For that is where the whale men
And the dolphin men hang out,
And they made their notes
And ecological plans and took
Blood samples and measured the tide
So that the whale now lies
Under the limestone reaches,
Proud steps to the summer storm,
Turquoise and shimmering,
Great sea mammal, partner of song.

We Sell, You Buy: Gulf War 1

We sell, you buy:
Exocet, Pershing, Cruise, what odds?
We sell, you buy.

We have reasons a-plenty, piled up like pillows
On the creaking bed of your desire
To see the earth crack like an egg
And pour itself into the empty cup of space.
We sell, you buy.

The world's on the H.P spiral.
If we make black snow we must distribute.
Sales distribution, input, output,
That's the name of the game.

Why can't you understand, you of feeble
Belief: 'That man can't possibly do this?'
Of course you'll purchase the brand new sun
That'll give you a tan without flying south
For the price you're prepared to give—
Freedom was the word I think you mentioned?

I once read a book about some old Jap
Who saw the shadow of his daughter on a wall.
By the corkscrew of fate he survived to tell the tale,
Went far away and cultivated carp.

S.A.D.

Winter is icummen in, / Lhude sing Goddamm
— Ezra Pound

The swallows pack up
And go.
Tomorrow the geese
Will come.
Inside the house
In the purple dark
The table
With its city of junk
Tells you
That winter leans on you,
Has nudged you through all
The tower and babel
Of the past months
When a kind of summer
Was. Now the table tells you
It's the S.A.D.
Stale bread, hard as a helmet,
Dregs of tea, the last teabag
Like a dead mouse,
Yesterday's
Half-finished crossword,
Tells you
It's for winter.

Who's for winter?
Says your man
Below, growing his house.

The Horse Protestant Joke is Over

There's a small church
By the Big House
Outside of which
The notice reads
Everyone welcome.

Two grinning
Millionaires
Have bought the Big House

And they will have horses,
And they will have jeeps,
And maybe ride rough-shod
Over the parishioners
Of the little church
Which says
Everyone welcome.

House for Sale
for Sophia McColgan

Still the house stands
In its rope of wind,
Small cenotaph
To the weeds of evil,
The stone of memory
A solid fortress
That time
Will not erase.

The children's voices
Under chair and wardrobe,
Between the cracks
In the lino...
The broken hinge of terror
In the swinging door
That swings over and over
Is the house's destiny

Till it crumbles in history
Unwanted, unsold.

Song

I gave a poem to my friend.
He spat upon the burning ground.
I said, *My friend, it's not the end,*
My song is better than it sounds.
But he said lately he had found
That matter divulged and matter penned
Created enemies all around.

I wrapped my poem up in lead
And threw it in his scarlet face.
I said, *My friend, I wish you dead*
For such a terrible disgrace.
But then he only laughed instead
And wrapped his Easter up in lace.

In the Out-Patients of St. Mary's Hospital, On the Eve of Good Friday Last

High on Reds, short for Seconal,
Drunk out of her person,
bumming fags—beautiful lady
of London wept for the crucified Lord.
He died for us, for me, for you,
Transfigured, tomorrow we'll toast Him with whiskey.
The casualty's slack lips tightened.
Her words, encrusted with slime and sentiment,
Banged the air like a fist.
She wept. She crossed herself.
Tears from her crazy Calvary—
The prescription got would rise again
In Wigmore Street—
The all-night drug-addicts' haven.
Perfection is easily gained.
Social Security pays—legal high,
Suicide, bets on the Derby—you name it.
She was foul-mouthed, loving and highly practical.

'The Act of Poetry Is a Rebel Act'
—Michael Hartnett

Possibly those inquisitive eyes
Grasped the horizon
Of his wonder gift,
Tell-tales of lift-the-heart
Follies—like addressing the statue
In Killtimagh of a brandy-shadowed
Morning: *No wars of mercy fought*
On his behalf. His waging, lonesome
As any poet's, playing the poker
Of 'See you, raise you' till its echo tumbled
From the kitty of common sense.
How well he knew
'The act of poetry
Is a rebel act.'

Precisely

Of course
All things are rich to me.
Precision, equally, is correct.
The muscles of a boy's back
In early Latin sun,
The line of a Bentley tourer
Parked in a Georgian square,
Not to mention the neck
Of a racehorse,
Money itself,
The ablative absolute,
White in the sun,
The cold of a cathedral,
The smell of a new tennis ball,
Couperin's *Lecons de Tenebre...*

Still, I have seen
The boy, the Bentley
And the racehorse.
I have felt money and the cold
Of a cathedral,
Have smelled the new tennis ball
And heard Couperin's
Lecons de tenebre.

But memory games
Make patches wear
In the heart.

Prison Poem III:
For a Friend Doing Life In Portlaoise

I walk the crazy paving, the path of lies,
The micro-chip of satisfaction,
And mingle with the funny-money men
Who gossip on the shoulders of the judges,
But I think of you between the intervals of pacing
Or silence as on the edge of circumstance.

And with twice and nothing of what they have,
The bastards.

I send you the white bird of attendance,
The swallow that left too soon, migrated South,
The simplicities of daisies under boots.

Remember Jean-Paul Sârtre and other soldiers of fortune
Who lived on the rim of existence and survived
The cinder that drops beneath the grate and stays alight,
The fish that lies beneath the shadow of the stone.

Prison Poem IV:
Written During The Hunger Strike, 1980

I do so want to live but my body,
Stringent in its monkey martyrdom,
Withdraws into shadow splendour.
It knows I am helpless now to order it.

In effect the delay in dying spreads
Flat and reflective as a mirror.
Voices of others at one remove
Deploy old friends, natives of my mind.
They argue, frustrate me with their insistence.

It's hard to see: motes of light tumble
Like tadpoles. I remember chemistry,
A cross teacher, the jargon of formulae,
How all could be clarified in the body-mortal
If only I paid attention.

Some days I am careless; I cope adequately
With skin and thighs. Feet, more determined,
Claim my attention as though
They braved the frontier without permit.
This amuses me. I admire them for their stress
Of personality. Allow them to peer from beneath
Their triangle of blanket. I would like to meet them half-way,
Acknowledge that their geometry is relevant.

On other days I am invaded by heat, my skull especially.
In this state my mind is laid back
For the repeated information of pain.

I do so want to live
Or is that someone else talking?

Dublin, December 1980

Two Poems i.m. Stevie Smith

The Girl in a Box

Once upon a time
There was a girl in a box
And her pretty china face
Was full of love.
(She never moved.)

Why does she lie there like that
Without moving, so frail, so spent?

Perhaps she is dead, they said.
And away they went.

Dear Mr. Psychiatrist

Dear Mr. Psychiatrist
I don't like your pills.
(I prefer my ills)

I am a doll's house
And my bricks are ruby red.
Mummy and Daddy are in my bottles
With pretty plastic phials of love.

Oh, sweet rainbow, break me.

The Bed Bug

I am a bed bug.
I am flat.
I am starving.

They say God didn't invent me
But I am alive.
Society has done for me.
I live in a matchbox.

Somebody invented me,
If not God,
So I can live indefinitely
In a matchbox
Alone.

I am alive
But they won't feed me.
I am transparent
But basically
I am a bed bug.

In My Darling Liza's Eyes

In my darling Liza's eyes
I see her father.
Her shoulders are square, like his,
As though she carried two buckets
On a yoke.

She leans over the bar and slurps her vodka.
Oh, Liza, do you hear that voice in your throat?

Four Woodbines

In the torn and dirty sheets of those winter years
Spent in my wet mac, clutching the green packet
With its fiery orange sash—four Woodbines—
And my mongrel dog scratching its pedigree of fleas,
I was happy as a child could be, hiding under the shelf of Confey.

Drunk from the spilling rain, the stumpy field
Shrank from the ruined church, the glue factory,
Four headstones, I remember, aslant and broken as winos.

The winter mists came early then,
Tucked up the river in a long white scarf

While, heavy with fish and water-hens,
It rolled on quietly in the textured night.

Two-pence halfpenny—old money—
Not much to pay in retrospect
For the healing wonder of that glorious leaf.

Mrs. Katherine Dunne, Street Trader, Camden Street, Dublin, Died March 1983

Three on the bottle! Just like me!
She gave me a pram then—did she remember?
Now I address her dignity—Summer and winter,
On the pavements of time. One day, too,
And I cold, she gave me tea as she stood
With snow on her lips and the shyest of smiles.

But that was a while ago now and the children
Have plagued and played us, as tombola and fife.
The bingo of life picks the strangest numbers
And drums up tunes in the weirdest dissarray.

In the lamplight of chat—how the country swings
(and not for us)—I'd finger the aubergines,
the wounded cabbages, the French Delicous,
Tasteless as electricity in their super-shine,
Happy to find an Irish Cox
Whose sweet juice runs on the tongue
And she'd say: *Ah, I kept that one for you.*

Not easy to be a trader all those years,
Summer and winter, watching the generations pass
Like camels on a video horizon,
And staying motionless as Asia, never growing old
Herself, just wiser and more beautiful.

Was she always waiting for that pain to come,
To call a taxi like a tumbril and say *Cheerio
and see you soon.* I wonder why I'm left
The simple pride of having known her.

If the Baby Powers we shared
In the rush and tinsel of one Christmas Eve
May not be drunk this year nor any future
Year, I'll gladly hold the gift-horse bridle reins
And wait for the pain to come to call a cab.

Nightmare

It is dark in my father's shoe,
His experienced shoe. I scratch my skin
On the buckle and the laces.

He crunches about
On top of me. Underneath his arm

He has a cricket bat.
He is waiting
For the next man out.

A Mother Mourns Her Heroin-Addicted Daughter

How could I have dreamt
That my bird of paradise,
My green-clad hippie girl,
Could be so reduced
To the gammon face of poverty,
The incessant whinge of a child.

If we rolled up time like a ball
I'd give you the cherries of my nipples,
I'd wash you almond clean
And lay your hair like lint
On the cartilege of my breast.

A prey to the barren street, you're lost
On the breach of years that no silk
Nor cotton drawing-to of threads
Can mend. The void. Your path is marked
Like gull-prints on an empty beach.

The drug has perished your will.
You float like a stick on a pond
In here, in there—to a harbour of lily-trees,
Or held for days in scum till the light
Breeze lifts you and you edge along.

Will you walk on my street once more?
I'll raise my pavements to keep you safe,
Open the balcony of my arms.
I will buckle your shoes again
And shine the mirror for your dance.

But you will not throw away your bag of tricks.
Your monkey fingers cling to the safety net

In which you nightly land, having walked
The trembling wire and heard the screams
Of anticipation, seen the up-turned mouths.

How can we meet down the glaciers
Of days, the furnaces of nights?

The Violets of the Poor

My muse invites me to forget my debts,
Pile up more enemies.

Invoke the few

Who are helpful, generous
But not always honest.
To make secrets for the few
Like "whispering time".

But the few are filtered
And numbered in the funerals.
They follow the coffins.

So I pacify my muse
By joining the cortège
And sprinkling my secrets to the mourners
Like the violets of the poor.

Black in Achill

What makes black so black?
Black soul, black Protestant
Black widow, black cat,
Black holes, black death.
So many blacks in Achill:
Dugort, Dooagh, Dooega
Dookinella. Black field,
Black land, black plain.
But what if, like a camera click,
The sun comes out
And shadows sythe
The mountain's umber skin
And gorse-gold sand?

Megan Fair Remembered, 1977

for Jacky and my three sons, Nicky, Eddie and Johnny

Crosslegged, she sits, the pregnant one,
Her boyfriend beside her. The flame of pride
Illuminates the cushion of his cheeks.
My sons throw frisbee beyond the circle of the camp,
A white knife skimming the shoulder of the field.
My daughter bends from me to whisper to the embers.
I finger the back of her hair, rising and falling.
Against the fire it is brighter than fire,
The colour of drenched apricot.
It ribs against my palm,
Electric, compelling.

In a pit, we have made this fire,
Scooped the crusted earth with our fingers
And lain criss-cross the twigs,
Ignited by sandwich wrappings, old newspaper,
Till the bronze flame entered the sides of the logs
And was comfortable, would work for us,
To make the grass a shade warmer for our thighs,
The skin tighten on our cheeks.

The children are fed first; my daughter
Has spread the cloth way back from the heat.
They are everywhere, like dark squirrels
Cupping their hands for the offerings she has to give.
Already the black pot bubbles—the soup slides quietly
Up the edges. Her limbs are loose and purposeful,
Her thoughts retain their cosmic pattern.

Now the fires are everywhere in the horn of night.
For a long time it was twilight,

A muslin of mist had clothed the landscape
But now the clusters of distant Lowry figures—
All at business with life—
Are at work, kindling carefully as we did,
Stitching rubies to the flank of the secret hill.

There is nothing to do now only wait
For the acres of feeling to be ploughed back into time,
A brief memory of others perhaps, the solid footsteps of strangers.
The Welsh, curious as bullocks about this Irish family
Or what we are wary of in the valley hidden below—
A suspicious village, a chapel crouching in its bed of meadowsweet,
Or the offering of the wine of oak leaves and mountain ash.

Printed in the United Kingdom
by Lightning Source UK Ltd.
109964UKS00001B/4-30

9 781904 556442